MINI HOUSES

MINI HOUSES

KÖNEMANN

© 2019 koenemann.com GmbH
www.koenemann.com

ÉDITIONS
PLACE DES
VICTOIRES

© Éditions Place des Victoires
6, rue du Mail – 75002 Paris
www.victoires.com

ISBN : 978-2-8099-1677-5
Dépôt légal : 2ᵉ trimestre 2019

Editorial project: © LOFT Publications S.L.
loft@loftpublications.com

Art direction: Claudia Martínez Alonso
Editorial coordination: Simone Schleifer
Edition and texts: Mariana R. Eguaras Etchetto
Translation: Equipo de Ecición

ISBN: 978-3-7419-2383-8 (international)

Printed in China by Shenzhen Hua Xin Colour-printing & Platemaking Co., Ltd

INTRODUCTION

The last few decades have seen a boom in the development of small houses in response to the reduced size of families, the density of cities, the demands of today's citizens and the rise in price per square meter of property. These small homes present the perfect solution for busy professionals, married couples without children and adults who want to live alone or with their partner.

Far from the concept of the last century, where importance and power were reflected by the size of a home, small houses (also known as 'mini-houses') have staked their claim in current architectural development.

In response to the increase in this type of small property, numerous companies and brands have created and developed products specifically for these compact spaces, marking a trend based on economy of resources and minimalist ideas.

INTRODUCTION

Si pendant des siècles, on a mesuré la position sociale et le pouvoir à l'aune des dimensions d'une habitation, la flambée des prix de l'immobilier comme des terrains à bâtir et la densité croissante de la population urbaine ont bousculé cette conception vieillotte. L'espace disponible en centre-ville étant de plus en plus restreint, y faire construire sa maison est également devenu rarissime. Autant de raisons qui expliquent l'engouement actuel pour les petits logements – urbains comme campagnards –, qui ont désormais leur place dans le panorama architectural contemporain.

Pour satisfaire cette demande, de nombreux architectes ont conçu des projets spécifiques, alliant économie de moyens et style dépouillé, voire minimaliste.

Le lecteur trouvera dans ces pages de nombreux exemples de petites maisons individuelles, où la recherche du confort malgré un espace réduit a conduit à d'astucieuses solutions d'aménagement comme de rangement.

EINLEITUNG

In den letzten Jahrzehnten gab es einen regelrechten Boom um kleine Wohnungen
– eine Wohnform die auf Kleinfamilien, die Einwohnerdichte der Städte, die
Bedürfnisse der heutigen Stadtbewohner sowie die Preissteigerungen des
Immobilienmarktes reagiert. Diese kleinen Wohnungen stellen die perfekte
Alternative für Berufstätige, kinderlose Paare oder Alleinstehende dar.
Weit entfernt von den Vorstellungen des vergangenen Jahrhunderts, in dem eine
große Wohnung als Statussymbol galt, vermochten es kleine Wohnungen (aufgrund
ihrer starken Präsenz im englischsprachigen Raum auch „Mini-Wohnungen" oder
„Mini Houses" genannt), sich in der aktuellen Architekturszene ihren eigenen Raum
zu schaffen.
Als Reaktion auf den Boom der „Mini Houses" entwickelten verschiedene
Unternehmen spezielle Produkte für diese kompakte Wohnform und schufen somit
eine neue Tendenz, die auf Ökonomie und Minimalismus gründet.

INLEIDING

De laatste decennia zijn kleinere huizen, als antwoord op de kleiner wordende
gezinnen, de bevolkingsdichtheid van steden, de eisen van de huidige stedelingen
en de stijgende grondprijzen, als paddenstoelen uit de grond geschoten. Deze
kleine woningen zijn een uitstekend alternatief voor druk bezette werkende mensen,
stellen zonder kinderen en volwassenen die alleen of samen willen wonen.
Hoewel ver verwijderd van het concept van een eeuw geleden, waarin het belang
en de waarde van een huis werden uitgedrukt in de grootte ervan, hebben kleine
huizen (ook wel 'minihuizen' of, op zijn Engels, 'mini-houses') hun plek veroverd
in de moderne architectonische ontwikkelingen.
In reactie op de groei van het aantal kleine woningen hebben verschillende
bedrijven en merken speciale producten ontwikkeld voor dit soort compacte ruimten,
waarmee een tendens is ontstaan gebaseerd op een beperkt budget en de ideologie
van het minimalisme.

INTRODUCCIÓN

En las últimas décadas, se ha desarrollado un auge de las casas de reducidas dimensiones que responde al descenso de las familias numerosas, la densidad de las ciudades, las modernas exigencias de los ciudadanos y el encarecimiento del metro cuadrado. Además, estas pequeñas viviendas constituyen una alternativa óptima para profesionales atareados, matrimonios sin hijos y adultos que deseen vivir solos o en pareja.

Alejadas del trasnochado concepto de que la importancia y el poder se evidencia en el tamaño de una vivienda, las casas pequeñas (también llamadas «minicasas» o «mini-houses», por su denominación en inglés) han sabido ganarse su lugar dentro del desarrollo arquitectónico actual.

En respuesta a la actual fiebre por estas pequeñas viviendas, diferentes empresas constructoras han creado y desarrollado productos específicos para este tipo de espacios compactos, marcando una tendencia basada en la economía de medios y el ideario minimalista.

INTRODUZIONE

Gli ultimi decenni hanno assistito a un vero e proprio boom delle case piccole in risposta alla contrazione delle famiglie, alla densità di popolazione nelle città, alle esigenze dei moderni cittadini e al rincaro dei prezzi al metro quadro. Queste miniabitazioni rappresentano un'alternativa ottimale per professionisti indaffarati, coppie sposate senza figli, single o conviventi.

Ormai libere dall'idea dominante nel secolo scorso, in base alle quale l'importanza e il potere si manifestavano nelle dimensioni di una casa, le miniabitazioni (chiamate anche «minicase» o «mini-house») hanno saputo conquistarsi uno spazio all'interno delle tendenze architettoniche degli ultimi tempi.

In risposta al successo delle minicase, varie imprese e marche hanno creato e sviluppato prodotti specifici per questi spazi compatti, manifestando una tendenza fondata sull'economia dei mezzi e su concetti minimalisti.

INTRODUÇÃO

Nas últimas décadas assistiu-se a um boom no desenvolvimento de casas pequenas, encaradas como resposta ao aumento do número de famílias reduzidas, à densidade das cidades, às exigências dos cidadãos actuais e ao aumento do preço do metro quadrado nos centros urbanos. Estas casas pequenas representam uma solução perfeita para profissionais com agendas preenchidas, casais sem filhos e adultos que optaram por viver sozinhos.

Rompendo com os conceitos do século passado, em que se considerava que a importância e o poder de uma pessoa se reflectia no tamanho da sua casa, este tipo de imóveis (também designadas de «mini-casas») têm vindo a assumir uma importância crescente no âmbito da arquitectura contemporânea.

De forma a dar resposta ao aumento deste tipo de pequena propriedade, um grande número de empresas e marcas têm vindo a criar e a desenvolver produtos específicos para estes espaços compactos, definindo uma tendência baseada na economia de recursos e em ideias minimalistas.

INTRODUKTION

Under de senaste decennierna har vi sett ett uppsving i utvecklingen av små hus som respons på familjernas minskande storlek, städernas täthet, kraven från dagens medborgare och prisökningen per kvadratmeter på tomter. Dessa små hem presenterar den perfekta lösningen för upptagna yrkesutövare, gifta par utan barn och vuxna som vill leva ensamma eller med sin partner.

Fjärran från förra seklets koncept, där betydelse och makt reflekterades av ett hems storlek, har små hus (även kända som "minihus") gjort anspråk på sin rätt i den arkitektoniska utvecklingen.

Som svar på ökningen av den här typen av små fastigheter har talrika företag och märken skapat och utvecklat produkter speciellt för dessa kompakta utrymmen, och markerar en trend baserad på hushållande med resurser och minimalistiska idéer.

HOUSE IN TORRELLES

Rob Dubois

Torrelles de Llobregat, Spain

120 m² / 1,291 sq ft

© Jordi Miralles

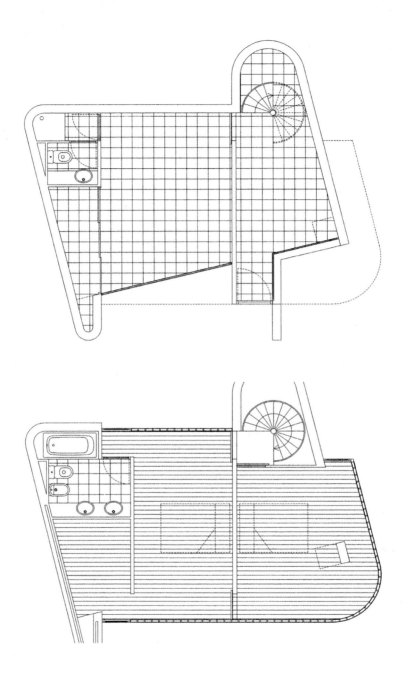

HOUSE ON MOUNT FUJI

Satoshi Okada

Yamanashi Prefecture, Japan

110 m² / 1,184 sq ft

© Hiroyuki Hirai

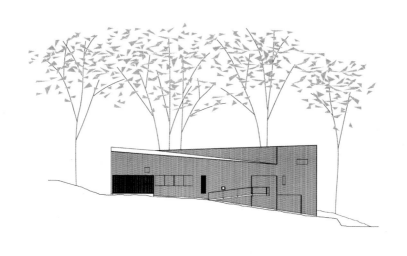

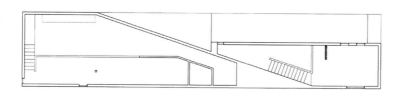

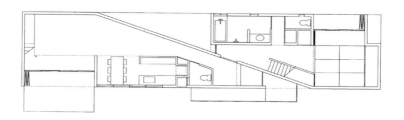

SUMMER RESIDENCE AND GALLERY

Henning Larsens Tegnestue

Vejby, Denmark

100 m² / 1,076 sq ft

© Jens Lindhe

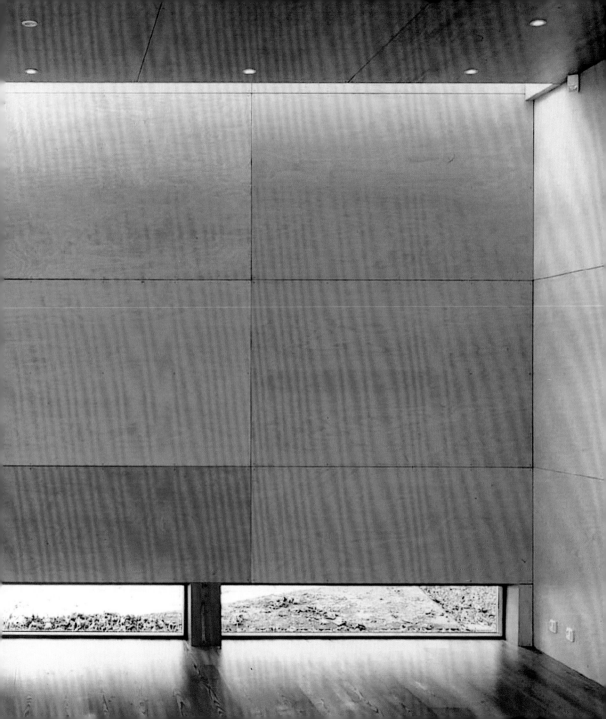

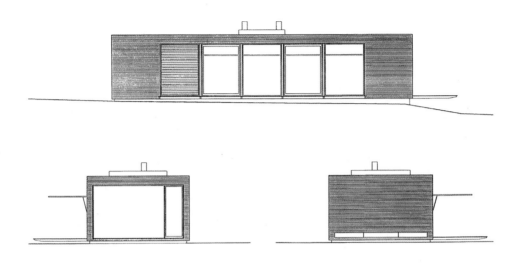

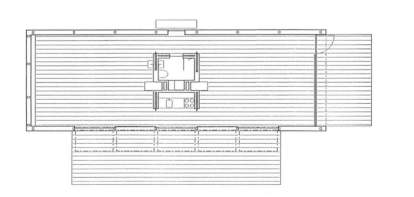

SOIVIO BRIDGE

Jukka Siren

Vammala, Finland

95 m² / 1,022 sq ft

© Lars Hallés, Arno de la Capelle

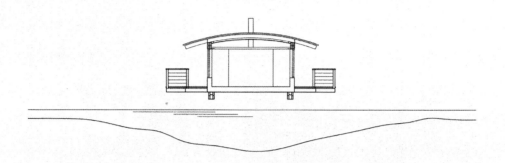

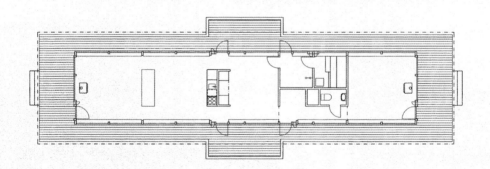

34

ITHACA HOUSE

Simon Ungers

Ithaca, United States

83 m² / 893 sq ft

© Eduard Hueber/Archphoto

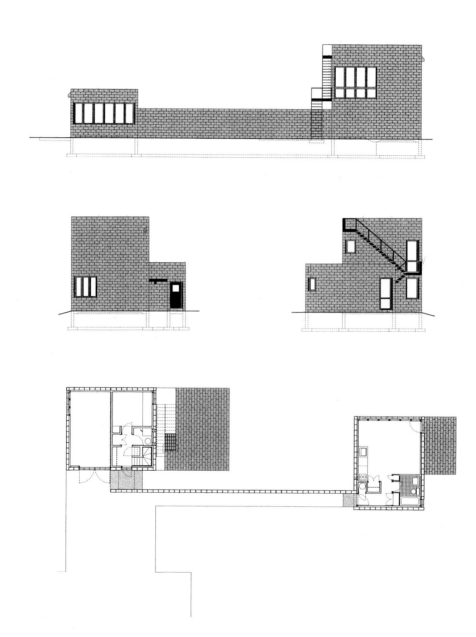

HOUSE ON THE ISLAND OMØ

Ole Holst

Island of Omø, Denmark

71 m² / 764 sq ft

© Ole Holst

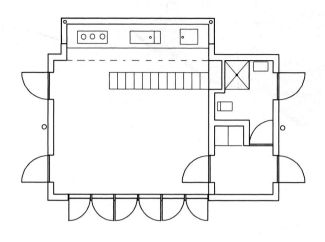

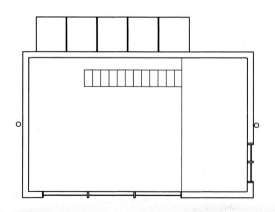

HOUSE BY THE SEA

Hanne Dalsgaard Jeppesen + Henrik Jeppesen Architects

Seeland, Denmark

77 m² / 828 sq ft

© Torben Eskerod

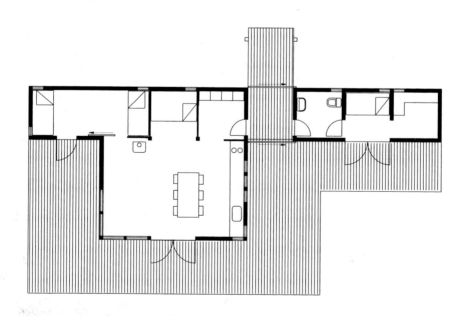

MOBILE HOUSE

Bauart Architects

Mobile

63 m² / 678 sq ft

© Andreas Greber, Haesle-Rüegsau

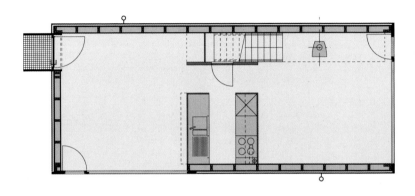

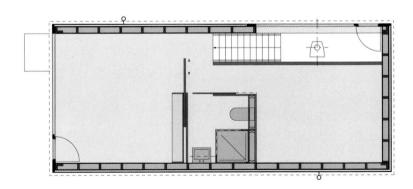

STUDIO 3773

Dry Designt
Los Angeles, United States
60 m² / 646 sq ft

© Undine Pröhl

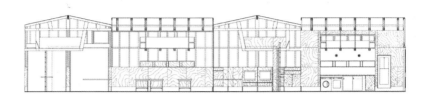

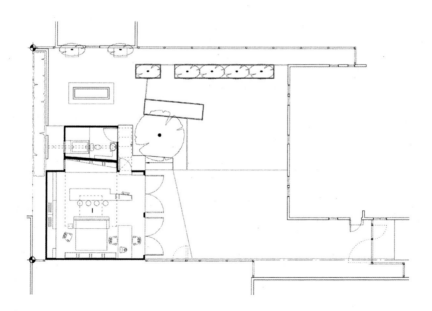

HOUSE IN ZACHARY

Stephen Atkinson

Louisiana, United States

51 m² / 549 sq ft

© Chipper Hatter

MINI HOME

Sustain Design Studio

Toronto, Canada

33 m² / 355 sq ft

© Sustain Design Studio

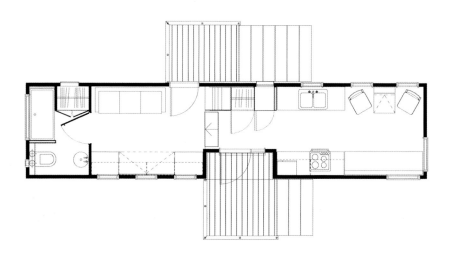

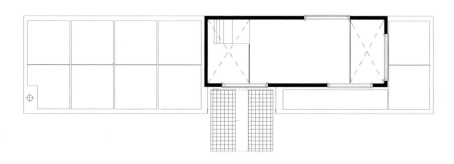

BLACK HOUSE

Andreas Henrikson

Halmstad, Sweden

33 m² / 355 sq ft

© Andreas Henrikson

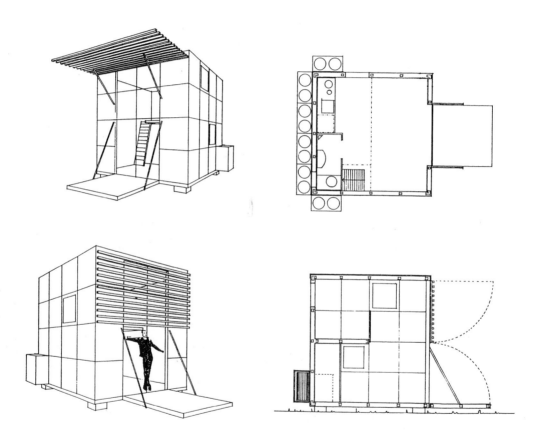

BALL HOUSE

Eduardo Longo

São Paulo, Brazil

100 m² / 1076 sq ft

© Fausto Ivan, Ana Carvalho

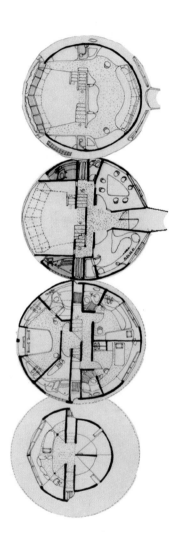

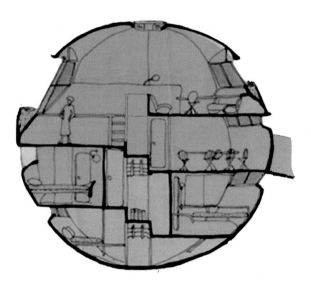

GUCKLHUPF

Architekurbüro Hans Peter Wörndl

Loibichl, Austria

48 m² / 517 sq ft

© Paul Ott

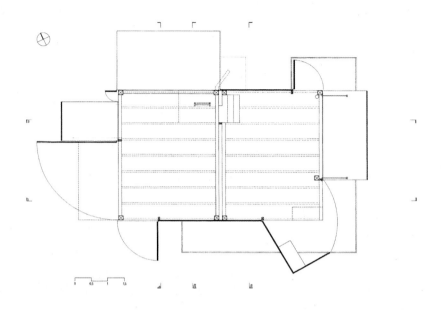

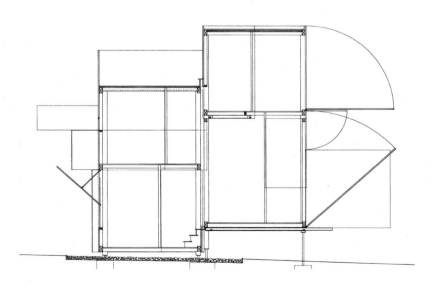

S•H•

Katsuhiro Miyamoto & Associates

Hyogo, Japan

103 m² / 1,108 sq ft

© Kei Sugino

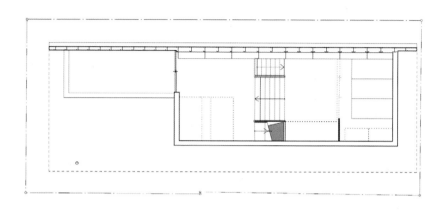

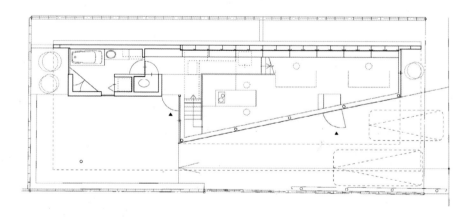

P•O•M EBISU

Rikuo Nishimori

Tokyo, Japan

117 m² / 1,259 sq ft

© Aki Furudate

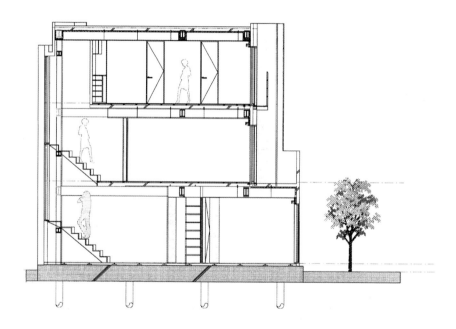

VILLA LINNANMÄKI

Risto Huttunen, Santeri Lipasti/Arkkitehtisuunnittelu
Huttunen & Lipasti

Somero, Finland

111 m² / 1,194 sq ft

© Marko Huttunen

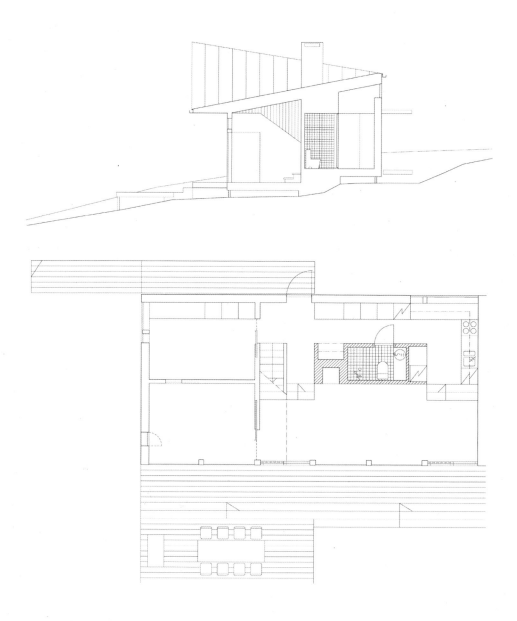

XXS

Dekleva Gregoric Arhitekti

Ljubljana, Slovenia

43 m² / 463 sq ft

© Matevz Pasternóster

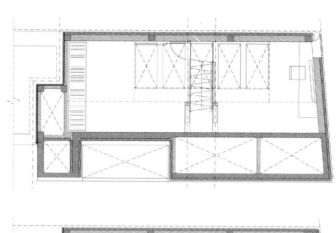

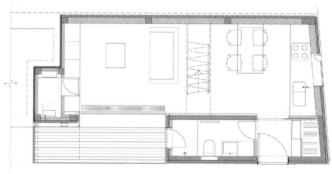

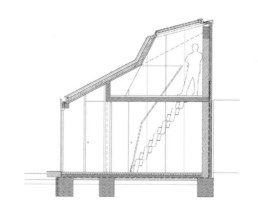

REFRACTION HOUSE

Kiyoshi Sey Takeyama

Nagoya, Japan

105 m² / 1,130 sq ft

HOUSE IN CHELSEA

Rafael Berkowitz

New York, United States

© James Wilkins

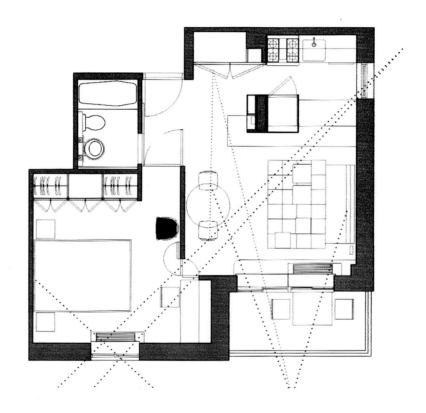

HOUSE IN MELBOURNE

Six Degrees Architects

Melbourne, Australia

80 m² / 861 sq ft

© Shania Shegedyn

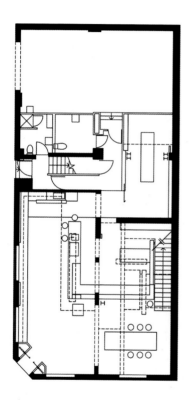

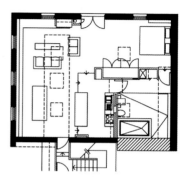

COCOON HOUSE

Michael Bellemo, Cat MacLeod

Wye River, Austria

68 m² / 732 sq ft

© Earl Carte/Taverny Agency

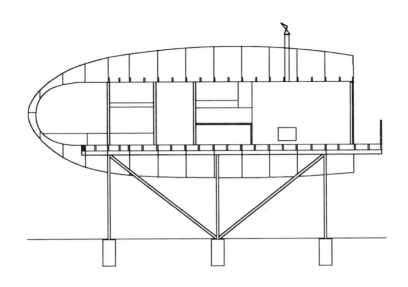

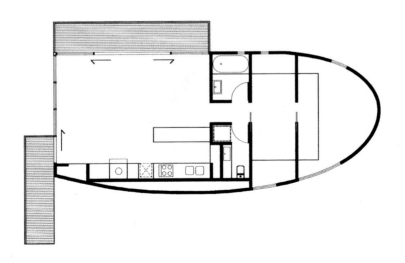

WEE RESIDENCE

Geoffrey Warner/Alchemy

Minnesota, United States

74 m² / 796 sq ft

© Douglas Fogelson

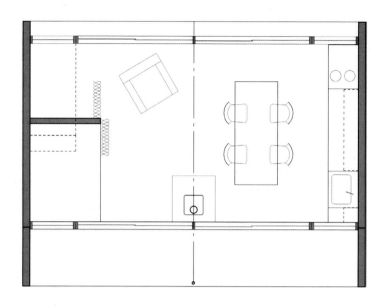

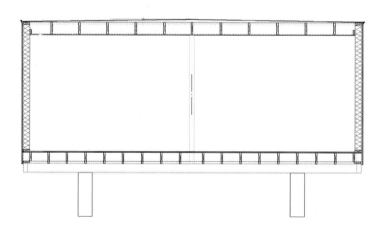

PIED-À-TERRE IN MIAMI BEACH

Pablo Uribe/Studio Uribe

Miami, United States

© Claudia Uribe

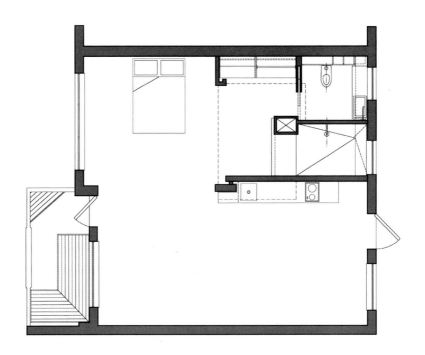

HANSE COLANI ROTOR HOUSE

Luigi Colani, Hanse Haus

Oberleichtersbach, Germany

36 m² / 387,5 sq ft

© Hanse Haus GmbH

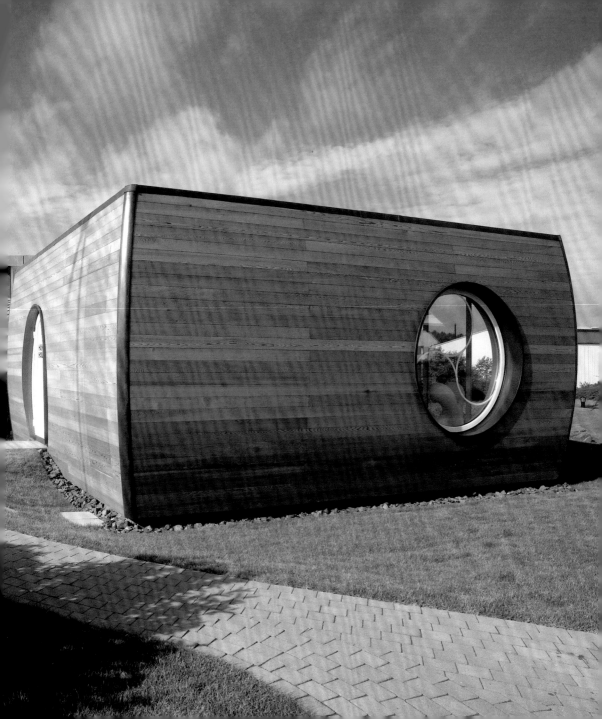

MICH MARONEY RESIDENCE

Michele Maroney

London, United Kingdom

© Carlos Domínguez

SLIT VILLA

C. Matsuba/tele-design

Tokyo, Japan

67 m² / 721 sq ft

© Ryota Atarashi

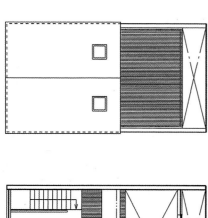

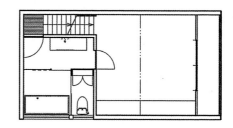

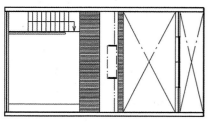

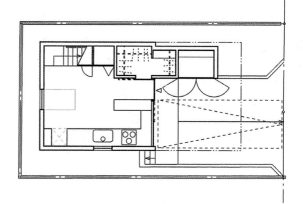

WALKING BOX

Milligram Studio

Saitama, Japan

78 m² / 840 sq ft

© Takeshi Taira

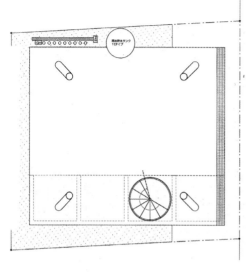

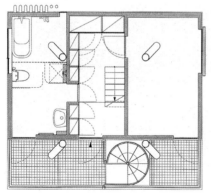

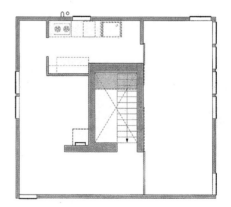

PIXEL HOUSE

Slade Architecture and Mass Studies

Heiri, South Korea

85 m² / 915 sq ft

© Kim Yong Kwan

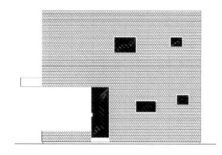
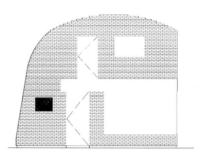

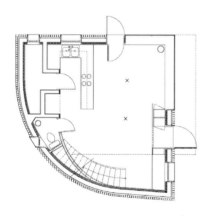
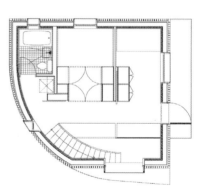

WHITE RIBBING

Milligram Studio

Tokyo, Japan

89 m² / 958 sq ft

© Takeshi Taira

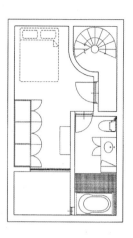

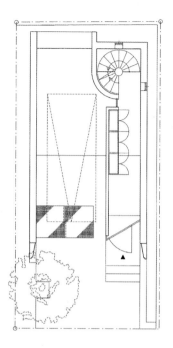

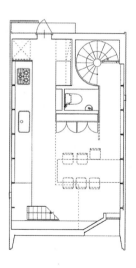

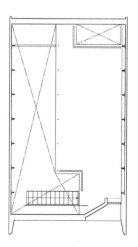

ROOFTECTURE M

Shuhei Endo

Maruoka-cho, Japan

95 m² / 1,023 sq ft

© Yoshiharu Matsumara

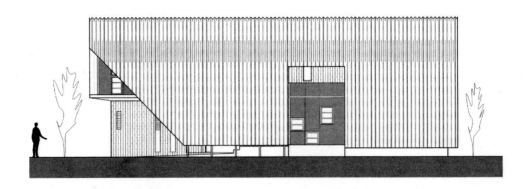

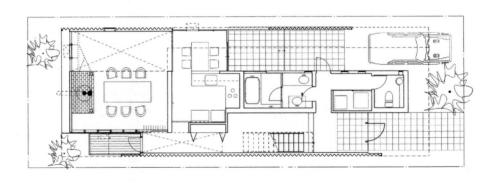

HEAVEN HOUSE

Flemming Skude

Lolland, Denmark

78 m² / 840 sq ft

© Flemming Skude

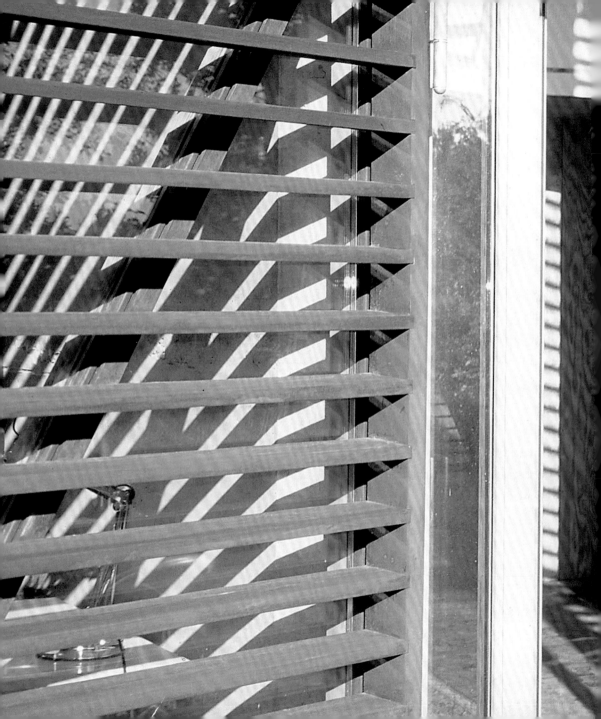

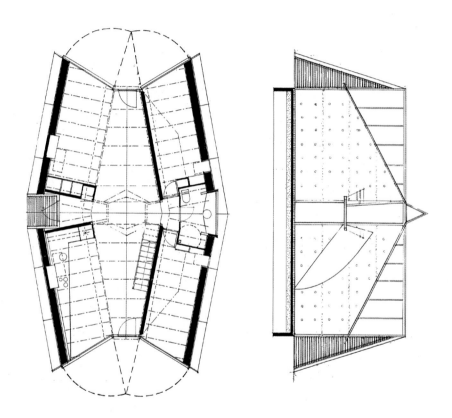

PREFABRICATED REFUGES

Geoffrey Warner/Alchemy

Two Harbours, United States

70 m² / 753 sq ft

© Geoffrey Warner/Alchemy

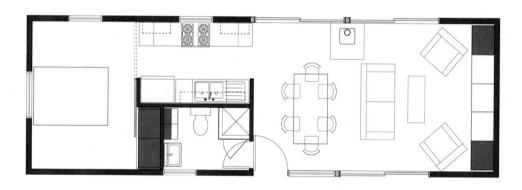

M-HOUSE

Michael Jantzen

Gorman, United States

93 m² / 1,001 sq ft

© Michael Jantzen

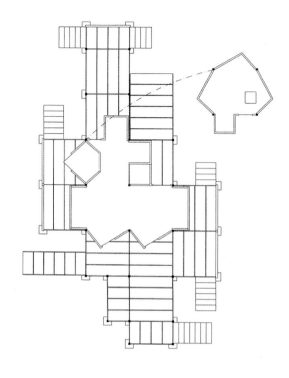

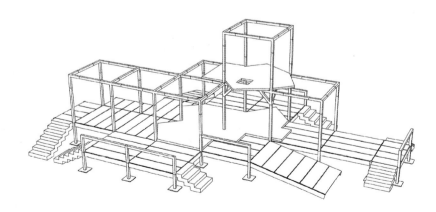

VERTICAL HOUSE

Lorcan O'Herlihy

Venice, United States

© Undine Pröhl

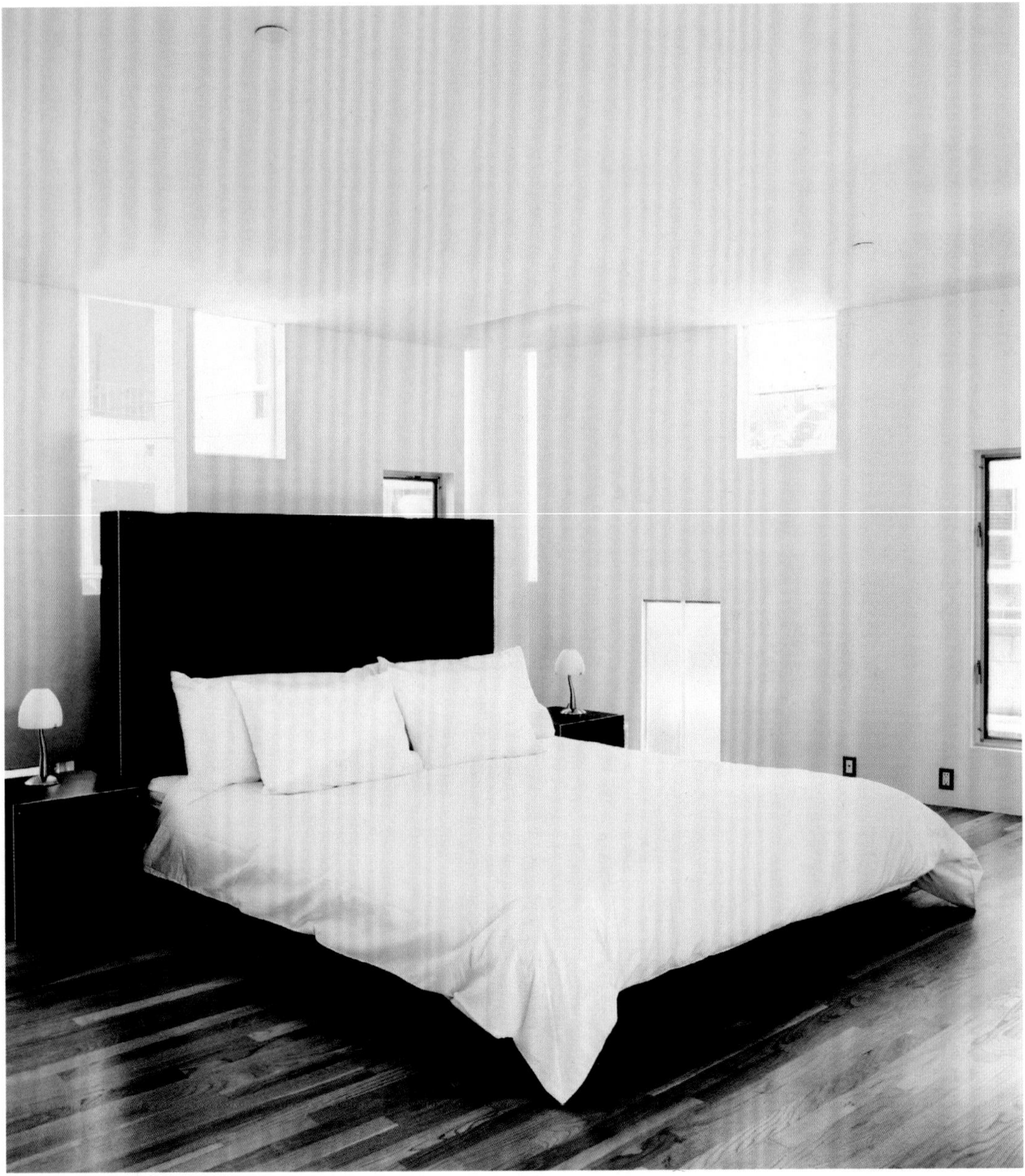

WEEBEE

Jay Shafer/Tumbleweed Tiny Houses Company

Mobile

10,20 m² / 110 sq ft

© Jay Shafer

SOCCER BALL-SHAPED HOUSE

Kimidori Housing

Gifu, Japan

50 m² / 540 sq ft

© Kimidori Housing

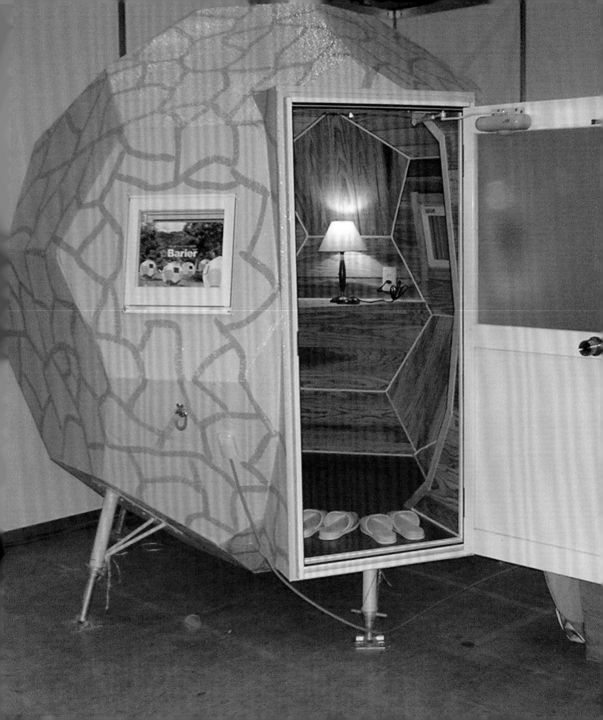

KITHAUS K3

Tom Sandonato & Martin Wehmann/Design Within Reach

Anywhere

11 m² / 117 sq ft

© Kithaus/Design Within Reach

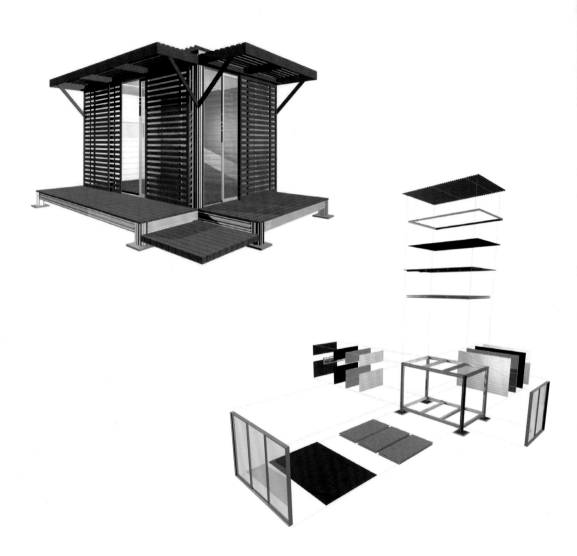

SEATRAIN HOUSE IN LOS ANGELES

Jennifer Siegal

Los Angeles, United States

© Undine Pröhl

RESIDENCE IN SYDNEY

Marsh Cashman Architects

Los Angeles, United States

© Willem Rethmeier

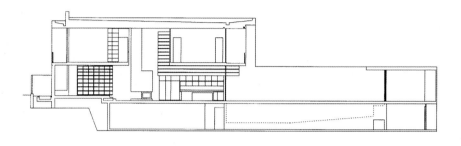

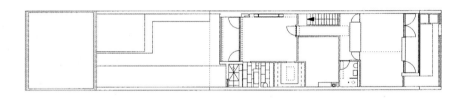

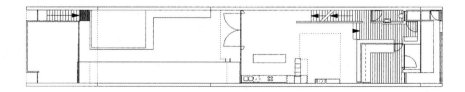

LAYER HOME

Hiroaki Ohtani

Sydney, Australia

33 m² / 355 sq ft

© Kouji Okamoto

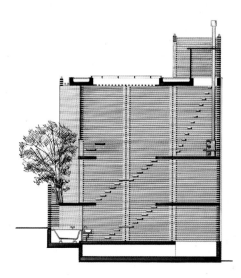

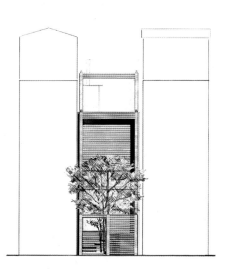

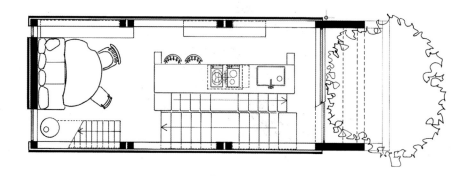

MINI-HOUSE

Atelier Bow Bow

Linz, Austria

27,40 m² / 290 sq ft

© Shigeru Hiraga

TELEGRAPH HILL RESIDENCE

House & House Architects

San Francisco, United States

© Willem Rethmeier

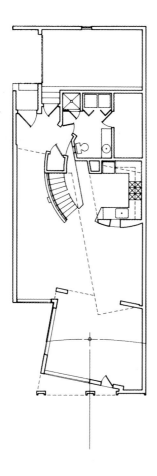
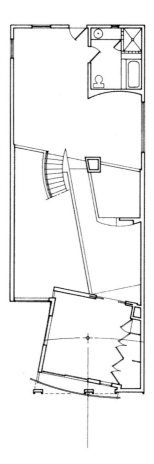

FOLD HOUSE

Mutsue Hayakusa/Cell Space Architects

Nagareyama, Japan

94 m² / 1,012 sq ft

© Satoshi Asakawa

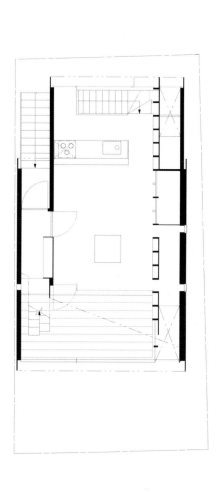

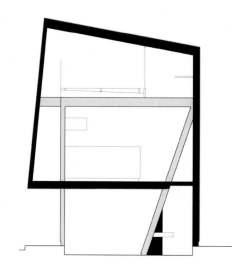

HOUSE IN SETAGAYA

NAYA Architects: Manabu + Arata

Setagaya, Japan

106 m² / 1,141 sq ft

© Makoto Yoshida

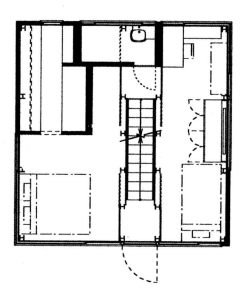

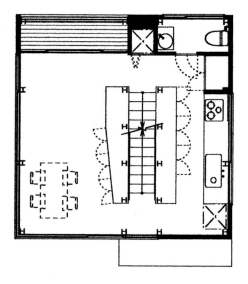

HOUSE IN MOTOAZABU

Mutsue Hayakusa/Cell Space Architects

Tokyo, Japan

112 m² / 1,206 sq ft

© Satoshi Asakawa

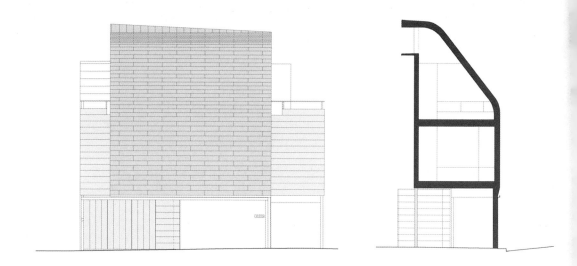

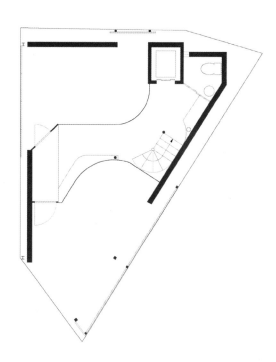

KASSAI HOUSE

Kiyoshi Sey Takeyama + Amorphe

Osaka, Japan

116 m² / 1,249 sq ft

© Koichi Torimura

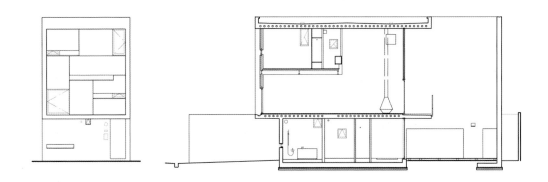

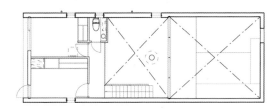

MINIMAL HOUSE

Ivan Kroupa

Mukarov, Czech Republic

72 m^2 / 775 sq ft

© Matteo Piazza

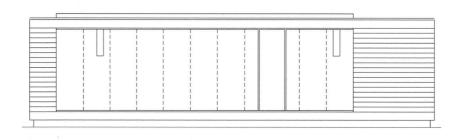

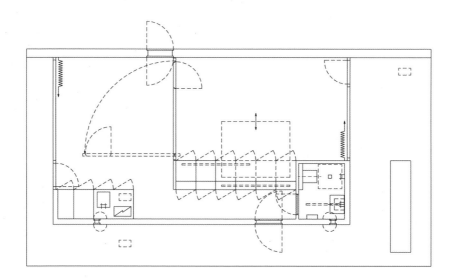

A HOUSE IN THE GARDEN

Archteam

Kromeriz, Czech Republic

75 m^2 / 807 sq ft

© Ester Havlova

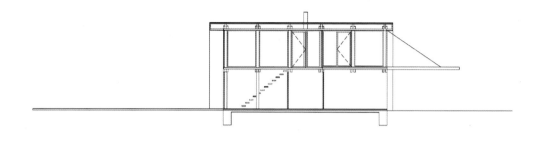

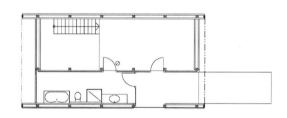

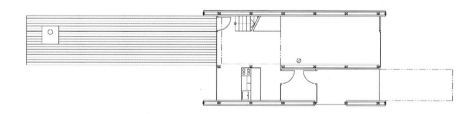

SINGLE-FAMILY HOME

Esteve Terradas

Gaüses de Dalt, Spain

98 m² / 1,055 sq ft

© Jordi Canosa

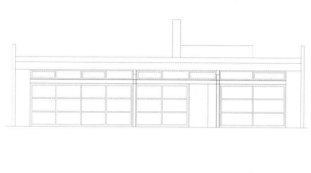

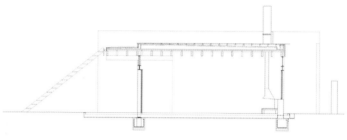

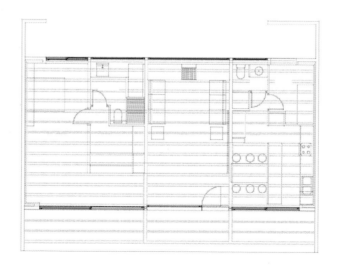

4X4 HOUSE

Tadao Ando Architect & Associates

Hyogo, Japan

118 m² / 1,270 sq ft

© Mitsuo Matsuoka

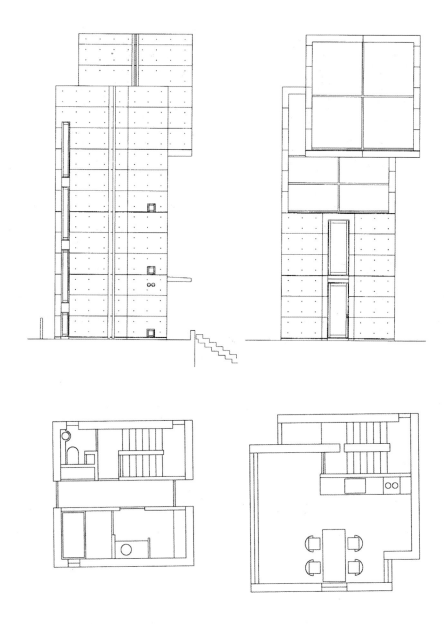

BOATHOUSE

Drew Heath

Sydney, Australia

35,50 m² / 377 sq ft

© Brett Boardman

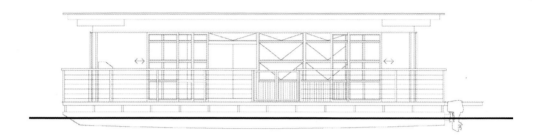

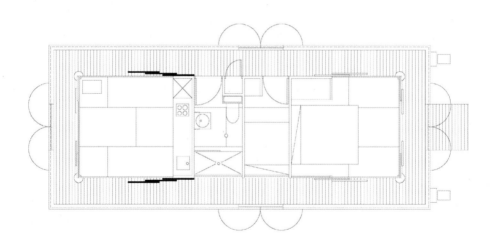

BOX HOUSE

Nicholas Murcutt/Neeson Murcutt Architects

Tathara, Australia

50 m² / 538 sq ft

© Brett Boardman

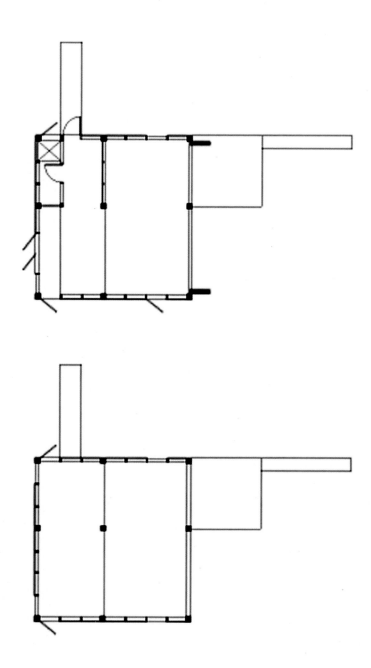

HOUSE IN CARRASCAL

Mariano Martín

Carrascal de la Cuesta, Spain

110 m² / 1,184 sq ft

© Pedro López Cañas

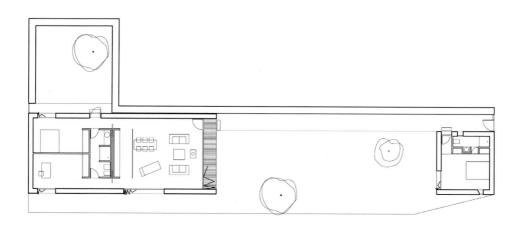

O-HOUSE

CUBO Architects

Matsumoto, Japan

62 m² / 667 sq ft

© Yasuno Sakata

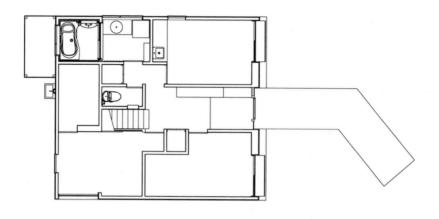

LOFTCUBE

Studio Aisslinger

Berlin, Germany

39 m² / 420 sq ft

© Steffen Jänicke Fotografie

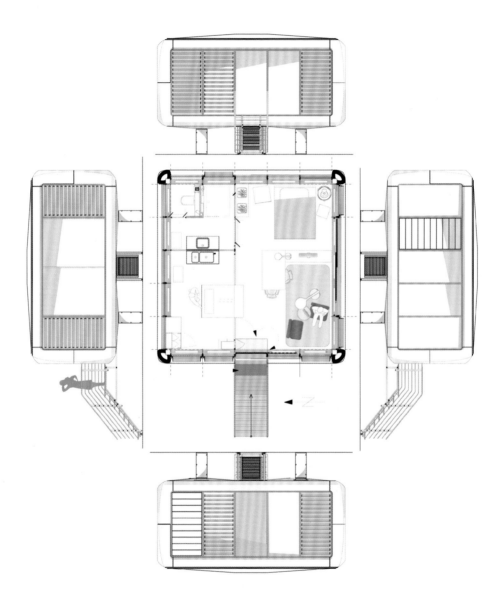

PREFAB HOUSE IN DENMARK

ONV Architects

Vanlose, Denmark

86 m² / 925 sq ft

© Station 1

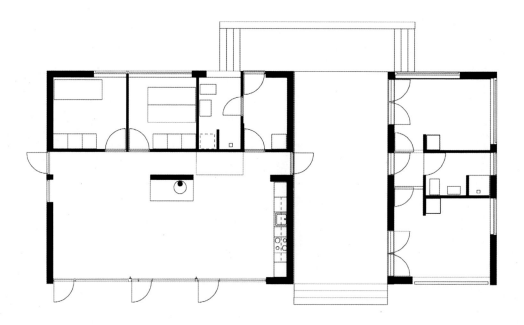

MICRO COMPACT HOME

Horden Cherry Lee Architects, Haack Höpfner Architekten

Munich, Germany

7 m² / 75 sq ft

© Sascha Kletzsch

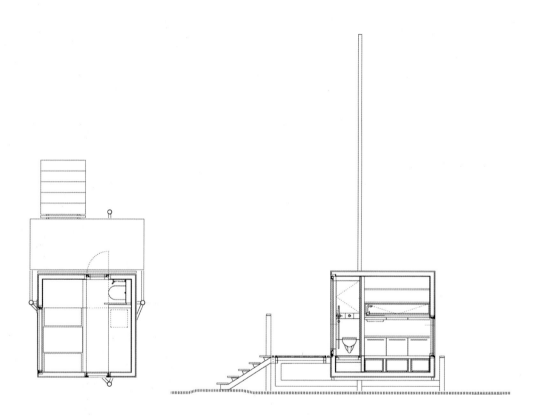

LAVAFLOW2

Craig Steely

Hawaii, United States

130 m² / 1,400 sq ft

© JD Peterson

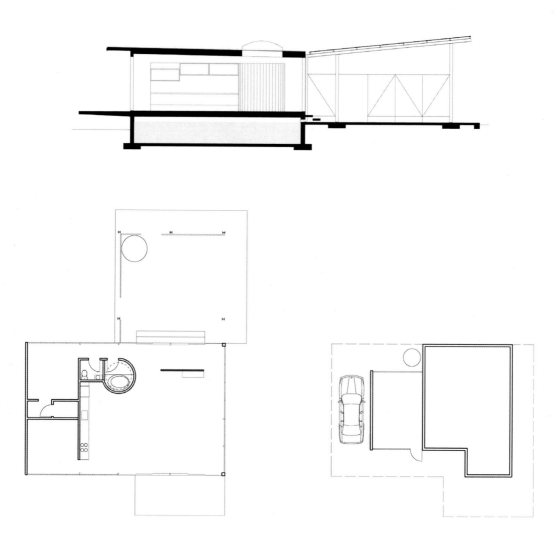

WINE CREEK ROAD RESIDENCE

Siegel & Stein Architects

Healdsburg, United States

© JD Peterson

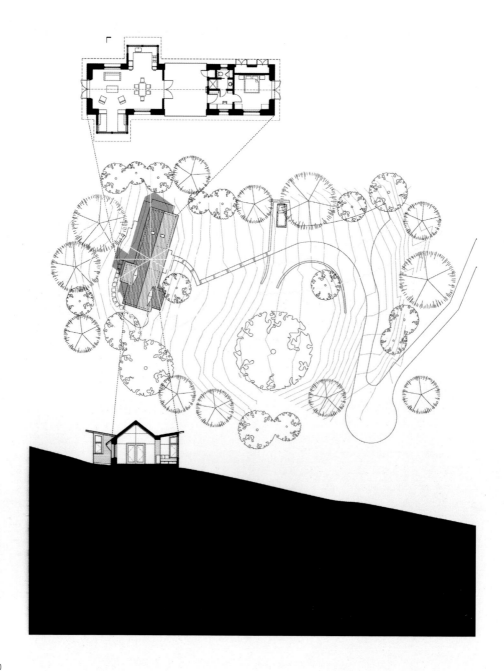

RUBISSOW FARM

Okamoto Saijo Architecture

Napa Valley, United States

111 m² / 1,200 sq ft

© Janet Delaney

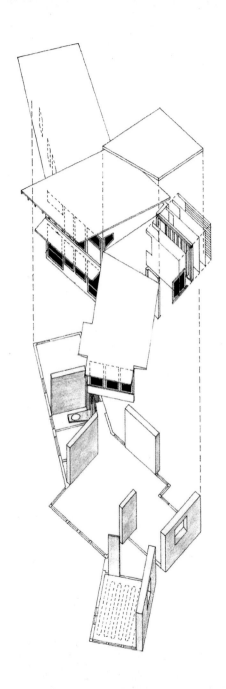

SOLARHAUS II

GLASSX AG, Dietrich Schwarz

Ebnat-Kappel, Switzerland

© Frédérik Comptesse

Flying Is Fun!

By Carol North
Illustrated by Terri Super

A GOLDEN BOOK • NEW YORK
Western Publishing Company, Inc., Racine, Wisconsin 53404

Ryan was excited. He was taking his very first airplane trip. He was going to visit his cousin in the city.

Grandma gave Ryan a big hug and slipped a little sack into his hand. "In case you get hungry on the plane," she said. Inside the sack were two biscuits.

"Good-by, farm!" shouted Ryan as he got into the pickup truck with Mother and Father. "I'll be back in two weeks!"

It was a long drive to the airport. As they got nearer, Ryan saw airplanes taking off and landing. "Is that the kind of plane I will be getting on?" he asked.

"Yes, I think so," said Mother.

Inside the terminal, they went to the check-in counter. The woman behind the counter looked at Ryan's ticket. She asked, "Would you like a seat by the window?"

"Oh, yes," said Ryan. "I want to see everything."

The woman typed something on the computer. Then she said, "We have a window seat for you."

"Do you have any baggage to check?" she asked.

"I have one suitcase," answered Ryan. Father lifted
it up and placed it on the platform.

The woman tied a ticket to the handle. "Now you're
all set," she said. "Here's your boarding pass. Your
departure gate is Number Twelve. Have a nice flight!"

On their way to Gate Twelve, Ryan and his parents passed shops and newsstands. Ryan's mother said, "You can buy one thing to take on the plane."

"I know just what I want," said Ryan. He chose a book.

Then they had to walk through the metal detector. Ryan had seen a metal detector on TV, so he knew what it was. "This is so the guard can see if I'm carrying something I shouldn't onto the plane," he said. He even had to put his little paper bag on the conveyer belt.

On the guard's television screen, Ryan saw Grandma's biscuits inside the bag. Ryan laughed. "They look like little rocks," he said.

When they reached the gate, Ryan looked out the
window and saw a big plane just pulling up to the gate.
His eyes grew wide. "Is that my plane?" he asked.

"Yes," said Father. "Isn't it a beauty?"

Soon it was time to board the plane. Mother said to Ryan, "Be a good boy, and mind your manners."

"Have a great time," said Father.

Ryan hugged them both and, with his sack of biscuits and his book, walked through the special ramp to the jet's doorway.

A flight attendant greeted Ryan. "Traveling all by yourself?" she asked.

"Yes," answered Ryan. "And it's my very first time up in an airplane!"

"I'll look out for you," she said.

"Would you like to peek inside the cabin and meet the captain?" she asked.

"Sure I would!" Ryan replied.

The captain showed Ryan the instruments on the panel and told him a little about some of them. "How do you know which buttons to push?" asked Ryan. "There are so many."

"I went to a special school to learn," said the captain. "And I've had a lot of practice."

The flight attendant helped Ryan find his seat and buckle his seat belt.

A gentleman sat down next to Ryan. "Hi," he said. "First time up?"

"Yes," said Ryan.

"You'll love it," the gentleman said.

The plane began to back away from the gate. Ryan waved to Mother and Father, who were standing in the big airport window. Suddenly Ryan felt a little homesick.

The plane moved into position for takeoff and then taxied down the runway, picking up speed. Ryan felt the plane lift off the ground. It made his stomach feel funny.

The plane began to climb. Ryan peered out the window. He saw cars and trucks on a highway. "They look like toys," he told the gentleman.

Soon the ground disappeared, and Ryan was gazing into clouds and sky.

The gentleman remarked, "Pretty, isn't it?"

Ryan pointed to a cloud. "It looks like my pet lamb back on the farm," he said.

Then Ryan opened his book and began to read.

After a while, the flight attendant came by and asked him if he would like something to drink. Ryan asked for some juice.

The flight attendant let down a little tray in front of him. Ryan drank the juice and nibbled on a biscuit.

Ryan asked the gentleman if he would like a biscuit. "My grandma made them," said Ryan.
"I'd love one," said the man.

Then Ryan decided to take a nap. He closed his eyes. He could hardly believe that he was actually going to sleep in an airplane up in the sky. He also couldn't believe how quickly the time went by. He had hardly dozed off when the pilot announced that the plane would be landing in just a few minutes. The seat-belt light flashed on. Ryan buckled his belt.

When the plane started to come down, Ryan's stomach felt funny again. He looked out the window, and through the clouds he could see the land below. "Look at all the buildings," he said to the gentleman. "They're so big!"

The plane landed. It took a few minutes to taxi to the gate, and a few more minutes for everyone to gather their things. Ryan was eager to get off the plane and find his cousin and aunt and uncle. At last the passengers started to move up the aisle.

Ryan spotted his cousin, Michael, waiting at the gate. "Welcome to the city!" said Michael. "Did you have a nice flight?"

"I sure did!" said Ryan. "Flying is fun!"